Edible Elms

He that eateth well, drinketh well;
he that drinketh well, sleepeth well;
he that sleepeth well, sinneth not;
he that sinneth not goeth straight through Purgatory to Paradise.

>William Lithgow
>*Rare Adventures, 1614*

Edible Elms

Compiled by
The Elms School

The artists sketches in this book are the work of Helen I'Anson
who runs The Elms' kitchen. Thank you Helen.

Edible Elms
The Elms School

Published by Aspect Design 2014
Malvern, Worcestershire, United Kingdom.

Designed, printed and bound by Aspect Design
89 Newtown Road, Malvern, Worcs. WR14 1PD
United Kingdom
Tel: 01684 561567
E-mail: allan@aspect-design.net
Website: www.aspect-design.net

All Rights Reserved.

Copyright © 2014 The Elms School

The Elms School has asserted its moral right
to be identified as the compiler of this work.

The right of The Elms School to be identified as the compiler
of this work has been asserted in accordance with
Section 77 of the Copyright, Designs and Patents Act 1988.

This book is sold subject to the condition that it shall not, by way of
trade or otherwise, be lent, resold, hired out or otherwise circulated
without the publisher's prior consent in any form of binding or cover
other than that in which it is published and without a similar condition
including this condition being imposed on the subsequent purchaser.

A copy of this book has been deposited with the British Library Board

Cover Design Copyright © 2014 Aspect Design
Original Sketch Copyright © 2014 Helen I'Anson
ISBN 978-908832-60-3

Contents

	7	*Introduction*
Autumn Term	10	*Autumn Church Service Lunch*
	10	Beef tagine with prunes
	11	Leek and brie tart
	12	Chocolate pistachio cake
	13	*Bonfire Night*
	14	Winter fruit salad
	15	Croutons
	16	Smoked haddock chowder
	17	Raspberry and chocolate waffle pudding
	18	Blackberry streusel muffins
	19	*Cookery Club*
	20	Parma ham, soft goats cheese, pesto and rocket
	21	Mushroom cases
	22	Rilletes of smoked salmon
	23	Potted prawns
	24	Spanish chicken with potatoes, garlic and sherry
	25	Thai minced pork in lettuce leaves
	26	Tom Rea's sundaes
	27	White chocolate pots
	28	*Christmas*
	28	Mini Christmas cakes
Spring Term	32	Crostini
	32	Mozzarella and marinated peppers
	33	Bruschetta with tuna, onion and black olive
	33	Broad bean crostini
	34	Chicory boats filled with pantzarosalata
	35	Artichoke heart and rocket mash
	37	Scotch eggs
	37	Sausages, honey and mustard
	39	Chocolate brownies

	41	Polenta cake
	41	Meringues
	43	Chicken gruyère
	44	Lemon meringue roulade
	45	Smoked salmon and scrambled eggs
	47	Sticky toffee pudding with pecan toffee sauce
	48	Chocolate croissant bread and butter pudding
	49	Citrus fruit brûlée
Summer Term	53	From the finest fillet of Elms beef
	55	Fried cabbage with juniper
	56	Spring salsa verde
	56	Crushed peas
	58	Smashed new potatoes with garlic and rosemary
	59	*Bastille Day*
	59	Escargots
	60	Normandy chicken
	62	Tarte aux prunes
	63	*Grandparents' Tea*
	64	Courgette and lime cake
	65	Beetroot cake
	66	Guacamole
	68	Quick chicken liver pâté
	69	Gazpacho
	70	Insalata Isabella
	71	Summer salad
	72	Elderflower and gooseberry ice cream
	73	Lemon posset
	75	*Speech Day Leavers' Lunch*
	75	Chicken with parma ham and goats' cheese
	76	Tomato tarte tatin
	77	Salmon in pastry with ginger
	78	Asparagus, pea and feta salad
Appendices	82	*Appendix 1: Weights and measures*
	83	*Appendix 2: Abbreviations*

The idea behind this book is to give you a flavour of The Elms School year and some of the events and occasions that are celebrated and enjoyed during the academic year.

Rural Studies is a popular subject. Many Elms' children when asked, "What is your favourite lesson?" will reply, "Rural Studies", with little hesitation. Active participation is encouraged and in May, as green shoots begin to sprout, a distinct element of competition becomes detectable.

Food is an important part of the day for a growing child. Being aware of the basics of food production is an essential part of helping to understand how produce arrives on the plate. We hope that Elms' pupils will enjoy turning basic produce into 'something special' and at the same time understand and appreciate the hard work that 'The Kitchen Team' put into providing their meals.

As well as the enjoyment of food consumed, mealtimes are a perfect opportunity for children to relax, converse and share their lives.

"Rabbits' friends and relations" have put this book together, choosing recipes from some of the popular meals that are produced in The Elms' kitchen.

We hope that you will enjoy reproducing some of these recipes, with the help of your extremely able and enthusiastic children.

Recipes feed six people unless stated otherwise.

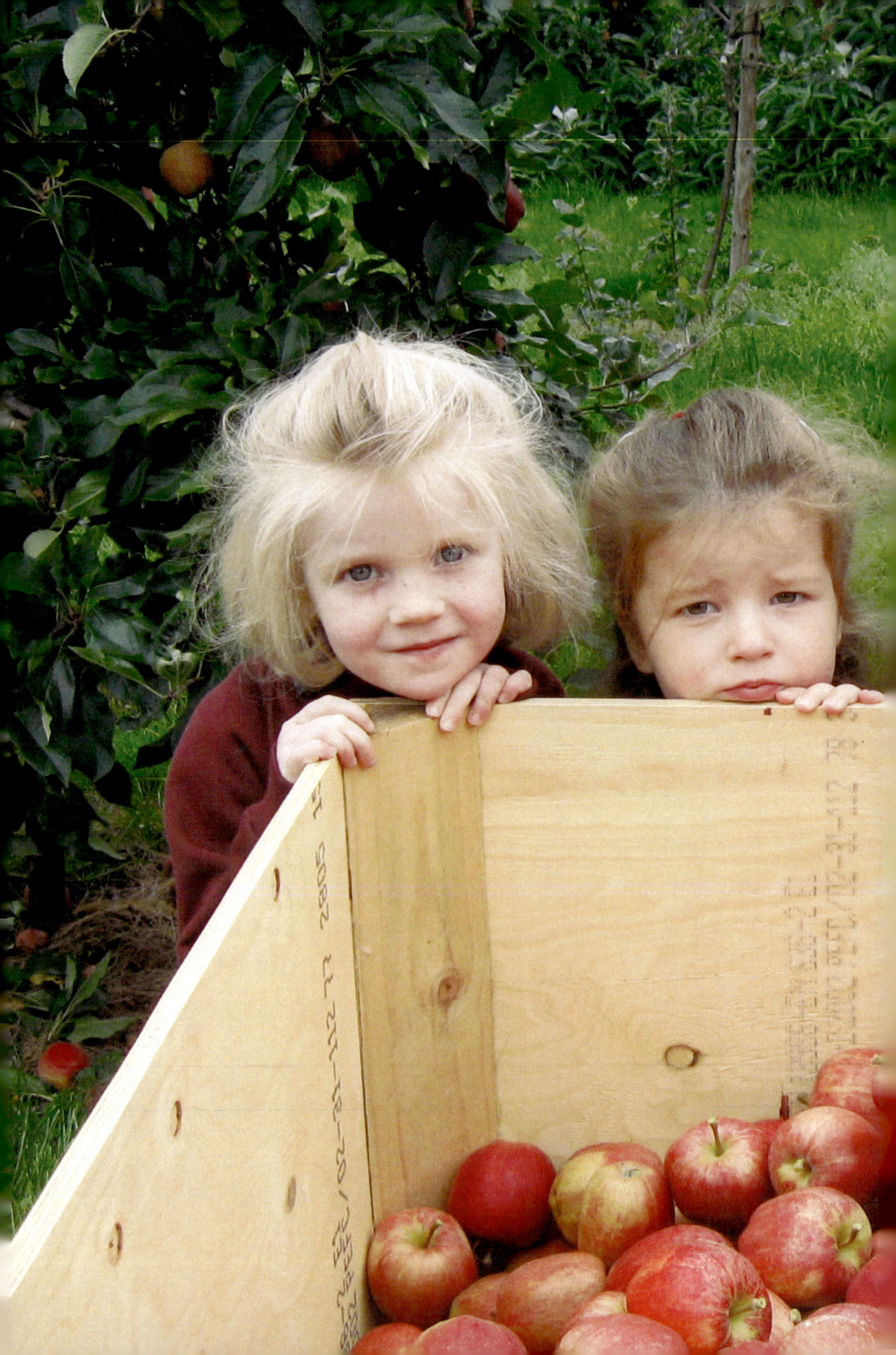

Autumn Term

With summer holidays over, The Elms embarks on a new academic year. Holiday adventures are exchanged, a new year of Pre-Prep pupils move up into the Main School and, after a long summer holiday, the children somewhat reluctantly return to the matter of education.

AUTUMN CHURCH SERVICE LUNCH

With autumn approaching and the anticipated season of mellow fruitfulness, the Church Service provides an opportunity for parents to get together and enjoy a delicious Sunday lunch.

Beef tagine with prunes

40	threads of saffron, infused in
2tbsp	boiling water
40g	butter
2tbsp	olive oil
1tsp	ground ginger
2tsp	ground cinnamon
3tbsp	onion, finely grated
4tbsp	chopped fresh coriander
1.4kg	stewing beef, cut into mouth sized cubes (fat removed)
392g	stoned prunes, soaked in water
2tbsp	runny honey
	salt and black pepper
	To serve
168g	blanched almonds
4tbsp	fresh coriander leaves

Heat butter and olive oil in a large pan, add ginger, pepper, cinnamon, onion and coriander.

Fry for 30 seconds, then add the beef, stir really well so that the meat is coated in the spice mixture.

Cover the meat with water and the saffron infusion, lower heat and simmer the meat gently.

Add half the prunes and cook for one and a half hours.

Add the remaining prunes and honey and salt and pepper.

Simmer for a further half hour or until the sauce has thickened and reduced and the meat is tender.

Serve with almonds (fried in olive oil until just golden) and coriander sprinkled over the top.

Leek and brie tart

8 filo pastry sheets
butter
6 young leeks (approx.), finely chopped
brie
2 eggs, plus 2 egg yolks
284ml double cream
pinenuts
1 tbsp herbs (your choice): parsley, dill, tarragon
salt and pepper

Preheat the oven to 180°C.

Melt butter. Line flan/tart tin with filo pastry sandwiched together (take 8 sheets of filo pastry and layer them by brushing with the melted butter).

Gently cook leeks in melted butter until soft – keep the green colour, don't overcook.

Fill the pastry case with leeks, then top with slices of brie and a sprinkling of pine nuts.

Mix the eggs and egg yolk with the cream and salt and pepper and your choice of herbs.

Pour over the leeks and brie. Bake in oven until golden brown.

Chocolate pistachio cake

150g dark chocolate
150g caster sugar
150g pistachios
150g soft butter
6 large eggs, separated
pinch of salt

For the icing (optional, but it does finish it off and make it more of an 'occasion' cake)

150g dark chocolate
150ml double cream
2-4tbsp pistachios, coarsely chopped

Prepare a 23cm spring form cake tin.

Preheat the oven to 190ºC.

Melt the chocolate in the microwave or double boiler.

Put 50g of sugar in blender and whizz with the pistachios until you have thick dust.

Add the butter and another 50g of sugar and blend. Then add melted chocolate.

Whisk the egg whites until 'peaky', then slowly add in the remaining 50g of sugar.

Pour/scrape the chocolate mixture from the blender and add to the egg whites. Give it all a fairly good battering and then pour into 'prepared' cake tin.

Bake for about 10 minutes at 190ºC and then turn down to 180ºC for the final 20 minutes or so until it is cooked i.e. slightly departing from the sides of the cake tin.

Leave to cool and do not ice until really and truly cooled.

Icing:

Put chocolate and cream for icing in pan and melt, stir, allow to thicken slightly (it will thicken as it cools). When the mixture has reached your favoured consistency pour it over the cake (it doesn't matter if it free falls down the sides), then sprinkle with chopped pistachios.

BONFIRE NIGHT

...sees Elms' sausages again, mugs of soup, jacket potatoes, toffee apples and gooey brownies.

Winter fruit salad

1 **orange**, peeled and sliced

large tin of sliced peaches

1 **lemon**, peeled – throw away the lemon and cut the peel in large slices in with the fruit.

225g **dried apricots**

tin of red cherries or packet of dried cherries

100g **soft brown sugar**

To serve

Few **raspberries or blueberries**

whipped cream or yogurt

Place all the main ingredients in a pan and bring to the simmer, then place in the oven with a lid for 2 hours.

In the last half hour of cooking add a generous slug of brandy or sherry.

Just before serving add a few raspberries or blueberries to liven up the look.

Serve with whipped cream or yoghurt.

Croutons

These are a great addition to salads or casseroles, soups... whatever is in need of a spot of 'crunch'!

2-3	**slices of stale bread**
4tbsp	**oil**
	salt and pepper
	herbs, to your taste

Slice loaf of stale bread in thickish slices. Layer up two or three slices and remove the crusts, then slice vertically and horizontally to produce small bite-sized cubes.

Pour 4 tablespoons of oil into a bowl, add salt and pepper, herbs if appropriate and toss the cubes in the oil. Coat the cubes all over. Turn on to flat tray and cook at 180°C for 8 minutes.

Smoked haddock chowder

50g	butter
1	Large onion, sliced
4	Smoked bacon rashers, sliced
250ml	whole milk
200ml	single cream
300ml	fish stock
1	baking potato, peeled and cut into cubes
200g	canned sweetcorn, drained
450g	smoked haddock (undyed), remove skin and cut into four pieces
100g	spinach, shredded
	salt and freshly ground black pepper

To Serve

2tbsp	chopped parsley, to garnish
	crusty bread

Melt the butter in a frying pan over a low heat. Add the onion and fry for 8–10 minutes until very soft, but not coloured.

Add the bacon and cook for five more minutes.

Add the milk, cream, stock and potatoes. Bring to boil, then reduce the heat to simmer for ten minutes.

Place half of the sweetcorn into a food processor and blend to a rough paste.

Add the puréed sweetcorn and the whole sweetcorn kernels to the soup and stir well.

Add the haddock and cover the pan. Simmer for 8–10 minutes until the haddock is completely cooked through.

Add the spinach and season to taste with salt and freshly ground black pepper.

To serve, pour into bowls, sprinkle with parsley and serve with crusty bread alongside.

Raspberry and chocolate waffle pudding

(6–8 People)

14	waffles (approx.)
200g	good quality chocolate
55g	caster sugar
1tbsp	(heaped) plain flour
3	eggs
1tsp	grated lemon rind
1tsp	vanilla extract
500ml	double cream
	To serve
2tbsp	(heaped) icing sugar
	cream or ice cream

Preheat the oven to 170°C.

Butter a medium sized ovenproof dish.

Cut the waffles into cubes and put half of them into the dish.

Top with half the raspberries and then half the chocolate, repeat the layers.

Whisk together the sugar, flour, eggs, lemon rind, vanilla and cream.

Pour over the waffles and set aside for 10 minutes.

Bake in the oven for 35 minutes until golden.

Dust with icing sugar, serve with cream or ice cream.

Another favourite recipe of the Pre-Prep is featured below. It is made by the Early Years after they have been blackberry picking.

Blackberry streusel muffins

300g **self raising flour**
170g **blackberries**
   1 **medium apple**, peeled and coarsely grated
150g **brown sugar**
   3 **eggs**, lightly beaten
80ml **vegetable oil**
80ml **buttermilk**

For the topping
50g **plain flour**
2tbsp **brown sugar**
1tsp **mixed spice**
30g **butter**

Preheat the oven to 180°C.

Make streusel topping. Sift flour, sugar and spice into a small bowl. Rub in the butter. Roll mixture into a ball and freeze until firm enough to grate.

For the muffins: put 12 muffin cases in a muffin pan. Sift flour into a large bowl and stir in the remaining ingredients. Spoon mixture into the cases and grate the streusel topping over the top.

Bake in the oven for 20 minutes.

COOKERY CLUB

Cookery Club is one of the after school activities offered to the Leavers' Year Group. Enthusiastic girls and boys gather round the kitchen table, a number of whom are by no means debutants in the kitchen and often have some original ideas and recipes to contribute.

Parma ham, soft goats cheese, pesto and rocket

1 **packet of parma ham** – 7 slices halved makes 14 'bites'

1 **tub of soft goats cheese**

decent quality fresh pesto

rocket

Remove a slice of ham from the packet and lay flat on board.

Spread a reasonably generous layer of goats cheese over a third of the piece of ham, then place a smallish amount of pesto on top of the goats cheese (depending on how much you like pesto).

Bunch up a small clump of rocket, place it on top of the pesto and carefully roll up from the filled end to the empty end (swiss roll syle).

With a very sharp knife gently cut the parma sausage in half, arrange with the cut end sitting on the serving plate and with the rocket poking out of the top.

Remember if you are doing anything that involves handling Parma ham keep it in the fridge until the last minute, it is so much easier to handle if it is cold.

Mushroom cases

- 1 box of 24 mini croustades (Rahms from Waitrose)
- 6 or 7 large flat mushrooms or the equivalent in small ones
- 3 cloves of garlic
- glug of double cream
- 6 or 7 sage leaves
- knob of butter
- Salt and pepper

Preheat the oven to 180°C.

Peel and finely chop mushrooms.

Melt butter in pan sauté mushrooms, add squeezed garlic.

Chop in sage leaves.

Add a glug of double cream.

Simmer fairly quickly so there is not too much liquid.

If there is too much liquid: whisk a small quantity of COLD water with 2 teaspoons of cornflour to make a milky mixture. Add to the hot mushrooms and stir thoroughly over the heat, this will thicken it all up perfectly.

Cool.

Spoon in to croustades cases.

Place in oven for approximately 4 minutes.

Rilletes of smoked salmon

(6–8 People)

large pot crème fraiche

1 **lemon**, juice only

100g **butter**

chopped parsley

10 (approx.) slices **smoked salmon (the size of your hand)**, torn in to large chunks

4 **fillets of fresh salmon.**

maldon salt and black pepper

parsley

To serve

toast or fresh bread

lemon

salad

Melt butter in pan.

Chop fresh salmon into bite size pieces.

Add fresh salmon to pan, stir until it is just coloured (1–2 minutes).

Add the torn smoked salmon.

Allow to cool.

Pour in crème fraiche.

Squeeze in lemon juice.

Add salt and pepper and chopped parsley.

Stir it all up fairly gently and pour into suitable dish… If you think it looks a bit pale, do the melted butter trick (as below) with some chopped parsley added and drizzle over the top of the rilletes.

Serve with toast or fresh bread, a large piece of lemon and salad.

MELTED BUTTER TRICK (Clarified)

Gently heat some butter in a pan, sprinkle chopped parsley over the salmon mixture and pour the melted butter over the parsley. Try to avoid pouring over the milky sediment in the bottom of the pan, this will achieve a nicer end look.

Potted prawns

450g	cooked peeled prawns (approx. 525g frozenweight)
150g	butter
½tsp	curry powder
½tsp	ground mace
½tsp	grated nutmeg
½tsp	maldon salt
	freshly ground black pepper

Spread the prawns out on kitchen towel to absorb any excess liquid.

Clarify the butter by melting it gently in a saucepan. Skim the white scum off the top and carefully pour into a clean measuring jug, leaving behind the milky sediment in the bottom.

In a clean bowl, mix roughly half of the clarified butter with all the remaining ingredients, add the prawns and mix together, making sure that they are evenly coated.

Pack fairly tightly into six pretty ramekins, small coffee cups, dariole moulds or one larger bowl. Place small bay leaf, or piece of dill, in the bottom of the mould. Spoon in prawns and press down to level the tops then spoon the rest of the clarified butter equally between each pot to seal the prawns.

Chill until set.

Serve lukewarm.

Serving suggestions – run the moulds under a hot tap if they don't turn out easily. Serve with lemon or lime wedges, fresh dill, cooked prawns, melba or hot toast.

Spanish chicken with potatoes, garlic and sherry

Lave por favor las manos (serves 4 People)

2tbsp	olive oil
8	chicken thighs
600g	potatoes, sliced
3	whole heads of garlic, separated but not peeled
2tbsp	pitted olives (conchilo)
	thyme, a good bunch
125ml	amontillado sherry

Heat 2 tablespoons of olive oil in a wide ovenproof pan which will take the chicken in a single layer. Season the chicken well and brown on all sides *(colour is important, don't cook the chicken, just brown it)*.

Preheat the oven to 190°C. Scatter the potatoes over the bottom of the pan. While it is still on the hob, add the garlic, the thyme and the olives, season, stir and make sure the chicken is coated in the juices.

Make sure the chicken is on top with the browned side up and add the sherry. Once the sherry starts to simmer, wang it in to the oven uncovered for about 40 minutes.

Cook until all scrumptiously golden and delicious.

Thai minced pork in lettuce leaves

1 tbsp   vegetable oil
200g   lean pork mince
1   red pepper, seeds removed, thinly sliced
1   small red onion, thinly sliced
2   red chillies, finely chopped
2   limes, juice only
4 tbsp   thai fish sauce (nam pla)
pinch   palm sugar or caster sugar
6   spring onions, finely sliced
1   small bunch coriander, chopped
1   small handful mint leaves, chopped
1-2 tbsp   thai sweet chilli sauce

To serve

1   iceberg lettuce, halved, leaves separated

Heat the vegetable oil in a large a pan over a medium-high heat and fry the pork mince with the red pepper and half of the red onion for about five minutes or until the pork is cooked through and browned in places. Drain off any excess liquid and set aside.

In a large bowl, combine all of the remaining ingredients, apart from the lettuce leaves, then add the hot pork and stir to combine. Taste the mixture and add more fish sauce or sugar.

To serve, arrange the lettuce leaves on a serving platter and spoon the pork mixture into the leaves.

Tom Rea's sundaes

(Makes 4)

tub of good quality vanilla ice cream

Chocolate sauce

110g dark chocolate, good quality (cocoa content over 70%)

knob of butter

2tbsp golden syrup

2tbsp water

fresh fruit, keep to two of the following:

cherries

raspberries

strawberries

pear

bananas

kiwi fruit

blackberries

pomegranate seeds

Stone, peel or chop the fruit.

Break chocolate into a bowl, add butter, syrup and water, melt on low in microwave (or in pan on low heat).

Lay alternate layers of fruit, ice cream and chocolate sauce in a tall glass.

White chocolate pots

200g best quality white chocolate
200g crème fraiche
200g thick greek yoghurt

Break the chocolate into a mixing bowl, suspend the bowl over a pan of boiling water and stir until melted. Avoid the bowl coming in contact with the water, let the steam do the job.

Stir the crème fraiche and then the yoghurt into the chocolate, mix until smooth, then spoon into small glasses or cups. Top with your favourite soft fruit, sprinkle of icing sugar and chill.

By the end of the Autumn Term the student cooks have collected a fairly substantial folder of recipes which they have all tried and tasted.

CHRISTMAS

Needless to say the Pre-Prep are particularly enthusiastic about 'all things Christmas'.

The Early Years love making mini Christmas cakes, which make an ideal present.

Mini Christmas cakes

225g plain flour
1tsp mixed spice
170g brown sugar
55g caster sugar
6 eggs
225g butter
1tbsp black treacle
1 **lemon**, juice only
900g mixed dried fruit
150g glace cherries

Preheat the oven to 180°C.

Grease and line 12 small baked bean tins, or you can use a muffin pan.

Cream the butter and sugar together until light and fluffy. Beat in the eggs a little at a time. Sift in the flour and spice and fold in gently. Fold in the fruit, black treacle and the lemon juice. Put the mixture into tins and bake for an hour.

The final night of the Autumn term is marked by a heroic effort from the Elms' kitchen in providing a Christmas Feast. It is always a very happy evening. The food is festive and delicious, and, when feasting is over, revels begin and the most ambitious 'movers and shakers' take to the dance floor.

One term down on the academic calendar and a New Year about to begin...

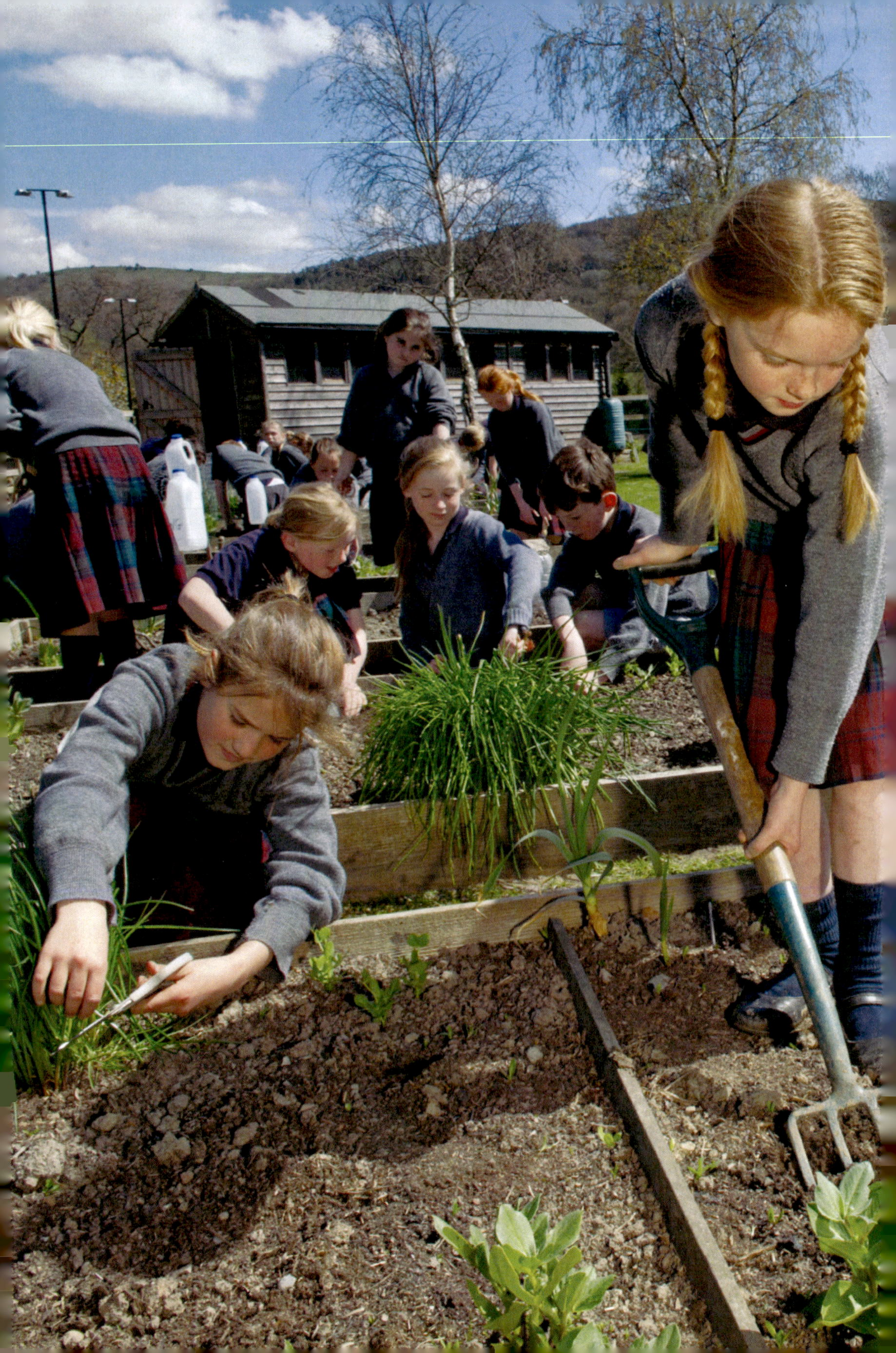

Spring Term

Crostini

baguette, ciabatta, or sourdough bread

olive oil

Crostini is a perfect base for any delicious topping that you may have handy. The base (crostini) can be slices of baguette, ciabatta or sourdough bread sprinkled with olive oil and either griddled or roasted on a tray in the oven at 180 °C for approximately 4 minutes.

Bite sized for canapés or larger for a snack lunch served with green salad – adapt to suit your needs and taste.

Mozzarella and marinated peppers

fresh mozzarella
1 **red pepper**
1 **yellow pepper**
10ml **olive oil**
chopped anchovy fillet
flat leaf parsley

Remove stalk and seeds from the peppers, slice the pepper into slivers and toss in olive oil in a pan until 'fairly wilted'. Allow to cool, then add anchovy and chopped parsley.

Season and prepare the crostini as above.

Place mozzarella on the bread, season if preferred, sprinkle with pepper mixture and top with a leaf or so of flat parsley.

Bruschetta with tuna, onion and black olive

Bruschetta roughly translates as toasted ciabatta. For a 'dainty presentation' the ciabatta slices should be halved.

1 **small tin good quality tuna**	Griddle or bake the ciabatta having sprinkled it with oil and seasoning.
olive oil	
1 **lemon,** juice only	Drain the tuna and mix with the chopped olives, a glug of olive oil and the lemon juice, stir in the onion and season if needed.
10 **black olives,** diced	
1 **small red onion,** finely sliced	
4 **slices of ciabatta**	

Broad bean crostini

150g **broad beans** (out of their jackets)

3tbsp **olive oil**

1 **lemon,** juice and grated zest

mint, a handful finely chopped, save some for finishing

salt and pepper

pecorino cheese, a few shavings

Make the crostini.

Boil the beans for about 5 minutes *(if you have time pop them out of their shells It will be a nicer end product)*.

Using most of the olive oil, pureé the beans with the lemon juice and zest, plus the mint, salt and pepper.

Spread on to the crostini, add a drizzle of olive oil, sprinkle with pecorino and slivers of mint.

For a lighter nibble which can be constructed with the help of young nimble fingers, chicory boats look colourful and would sit well on a plate alongside other nibbles, such as, hummus and pitta or flatbread.

Chicory boats filled with pantzarosalata

1 large beetroot
4tbsp chopped walnuts
30g stale breadcrumbs
1 garlic clove
6tbsp olive oil
4tsp red wine vinegar
½tsp salt
3 heads of chicory

Cook the beetroot in gently boiling water for approximately 40 minutes until just soft.

Drain, cool and, when cool enough, peel. Chop fairly coarsely.

Put beetroot in the food processor with all the other ingredients, apart from the chicory, and blend until smooth.

Separate the chicory into individual leaves, spoon a little of the beetroot mixture into each chicory leaf and arrange on a flatish plate with other nibbles.

Artichoke heart and rocket mash

- 1 tub/box of grilled artichoke hearts
- 100g rocket leaves
- 300ml olive oil
- 1tbsp toasted pine nuts
- 2 hard boiled eggs, yolks grated
- **salt and pepper**
- **olives / chopped parsley** (optional to decorate)

This can be made a day in advance if kept covered in the fridge.

Empty artichoke hearts into the blender, add all other ingredients plus some salt and pepper and process until mixed, but not broken down into a smooth purée, there should be plenty of texture.

Serve with flatbread or your favourite dipping option, adding a chopped parsley sprinkle for colour perhaps.

The meet of the Ledbury Hunt at The Elms each spring creates a happy diversion for both children and (to a lesser extent!) staff.

Mulled wine is handed out to the happy hunters accompanied by some warming morsels — two of which are courtesy of The Elms' Pigs.

Scotch eggs

(a Headmaster's favourite)

good sausage meat

herbs and flavourings of choice

boiled eggs... not boiled for too long – approx. 5 minutes – then cooled and peeled.

eggs, beaten

breadcrumbs

sunflower oil

Place the sausage meat in a bowl and add herbs etc. Take a ball of sausage meat and flatten it in the palm of your hand. Sit the peeled egg in the centre and mould the sausage meat around it, making a ball. Have a plate of breadcrumbs and a bowl of beaten egg ready. Dip the ball into the egg and then into the breadcrumbs *(it helps to keep the right hand for dipping in the beaten egg and the left hand for placing in the breadcrumbs... otherwise you get in a real mess)*.

Heat sunflower oil in a frying pan or deep fat fryer, gently cook the scotch eggs until golden and evenly cooked. Cool.

Sausages, honey and mustard

good quality sausages

1 tbsp **wholegrain mustard**

2 tbsp **clear honey**

2 tbsp **soy sauce**

Place sausages in a baking pan, cook at 180°C until they are starting to brown (approximately 10 minutes).

Mix the wholegrain mustard, clear honey and soy sauce together. Pour mixture over the sausages and return to the oven for a further 10 minutes, stirring and turning from time to time.

Another event in the Spring Term is Mother's Day Tea. This is always well attended. As with 'Match Teas', the popularity of the sandwiches and cakes that emerge from the kitchen is well evidenced by their enthusiastic consumption.

There is no reason why any of the following can't be used as a pudding or added to a picnic hamper to create a special 'buzz'.

Chocolate brownies
Makes 48

375g	butter
375g	good dark chocolate
6	eggs
250g	caster sugar
250g	muscavado brown sugar
225g	plain flour
1tsp	salt
1tbsp	vanilla extract

Preheat the oven to 180°C.

Line a flattish pan with baking parchment.

Melt butter and chocolate gently in a heavy based pan, leave to cool.

Beat eggs with sugar and vanilla, add the chocolate mixture and beat in the flour. Pour onto baking tray/tin. Bake for 25 minutes.

Remember that Brownies continue to cook as they cool, so they should be soft and 'gooeyish' when removed from the oven.

FREE RANGE EGGS
...AND CHILDREN

Polenta cake

28cm	spring form tin, lined with parchment paper
500g	butter
500g	caster sugar
6	eggs large
250g	instant polenta
500g	ground almonds
4	lemons
1tsp	good quality vanilla extract

Preheat oven to 160°C.

Cream butter and sugar.

Add eggs gradually.

Add juice of one lemon and zest of all 4 lemons.

Add polenta and almonds and fold in.

Place on tray as the butter leaks.

Bake for approximately 1 hour till golden and just firm.

Meringues

Mini meringues filled with almost anything: raspberries and cream, strawberries and cream, lemon curd and finely zested orange peel…

6	egg whites
335g	caster sugar
	your choice of filling

Preheat the oven to 100°C.

Whisk and Dribble! The secret of a perfect meringue with a gooey centre is achieved by slowly adding the sugar to the stiffly beaten egg whites, dribbling in a little at a time.

Teaspoon the whites into bite sized blobs, then place on parchment paper lined trays. Cook for approximately half an hour, cool on racks and fill with whatever you like.

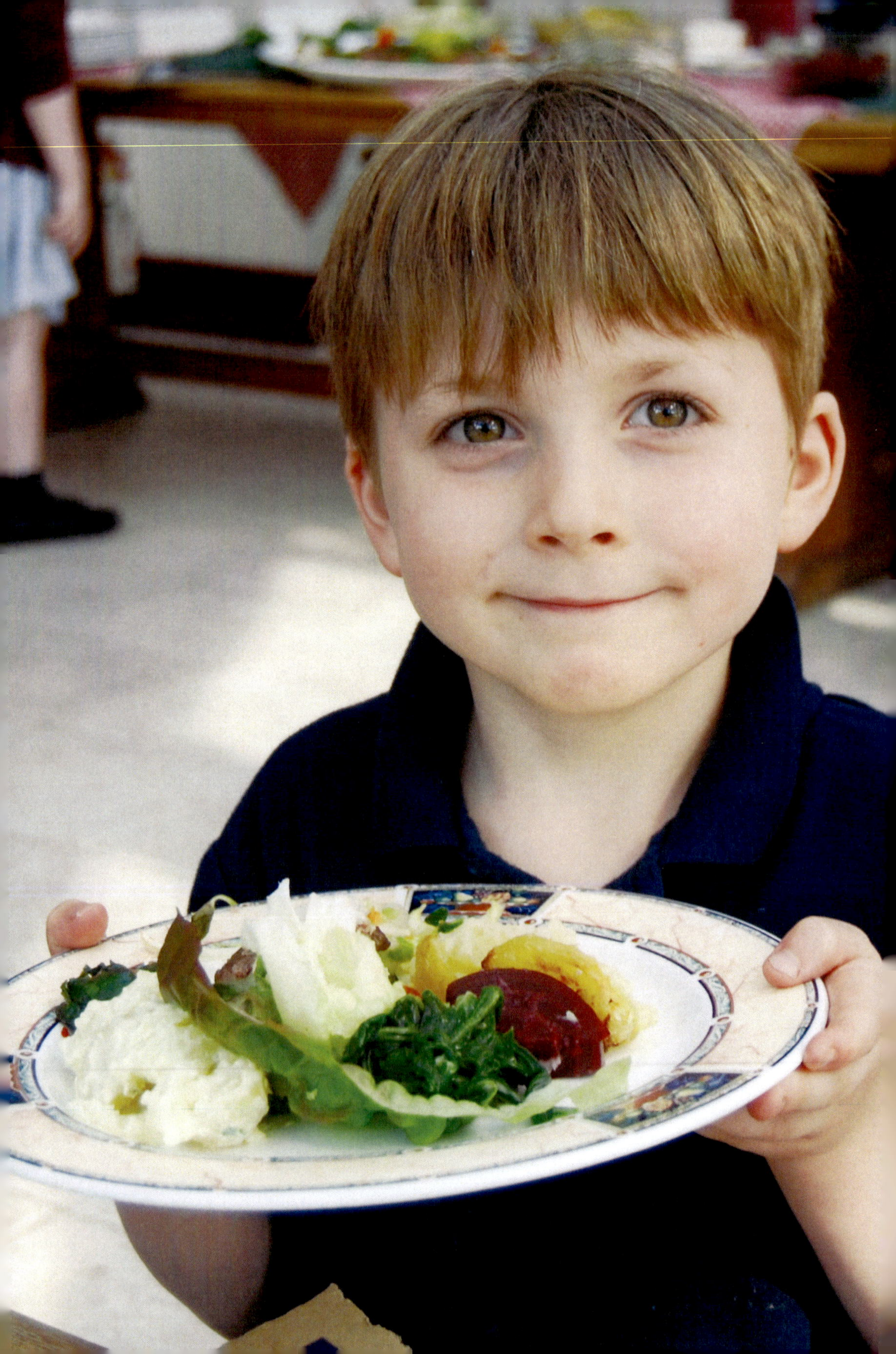

Chicken gruyère

- 1 **free range** (and very happy) **chicken**
- 2 **handfuls button mushrooms**
- 225g (approx.) **gruyère cheese**, grated
- 1 **large handful of chopped curly parsley**

Bechamel sauce

- 50g **butter**
- 2tbsp **flour**
- **milk** (add until creamy)

Poach the chicken in stock using onion and herbs (add any spare white wine that needs finishing).

Allow chicken to cool slightly, take the meat off the bone and layer up the chicken in a gratin dish, mixing in the finely sliced mushrooms and the parsley.

Make the bechamel sauce adding salt and pepper and remove the pan from the heat pronto zippo! Then add the grated gruyère.

Pour the sauce over the chicken mixture and cook at 170°C until golden and bubbling.

A green salad and freshly dug new potatoes are perfect plate partners.

Lemon meringue roulade

- 6 egg whites
- 335g caster sugar
- 4tsp cornflour
- 2tsp white wine vinegar
- 4tbsp (approx.) lemon curd, good quality
- 200ml (approx.) double cream (whipped but not stiff)
- icing sugar

Stiffly beat the egg whites then add the sugar a little at a time in a fine stream with the beater going. Then add the cornflour and the white wine vinegar to give a thick mixture.

Line a swiss roll tin with baking parchment and pour the egg white mix into the tin.

Cook at 120°C until firm on top.

When the meringue base is totally cold, turn it out onto a sheet of tin foil which you have sprinkled with icing sugar.

Spread the lemon curd on the top followed by a thick layer of whipped double cream.

Using the foil, roll the meringue into a round log shape; it really doesn't matter if it cracks.

Transfer to a serving plate and sieve over icing sugar (covering any craters that may have developed in the rolling).

If you don't want to use lemon curd, use any soft fruit.

Smoked salmon and scrambled eggs
(Brunch)

eggs
butter
salt and pepper
smoked salmon
sourdough, toasted

Lightly scramble some eggs with a reasonable dollop of butter and salt and pepper, tear up strips of smoked salmon and add them just as the egg is cooked, serve with warm toast… ideally sourdough.

The Spring Term is invariably cold and wet. Comfort food, although not entirely healthy, does provide some much appreciated seasonal cheer (in small portions).

Sticky toffee pudding with pecan toffee sauce

168g	**dates**, stoned chopped
175ml	**boiling water**
½tsp	**vanilla extract**
2tsp	**coffee essence**
¾tsp	**bicarbonate of soda**
85g	**butter**
140g	**caster sugar**
2	**large eggs**, beaten
168g	**self raising flour**, sifted

For the sauce

28g	**chopped pecan nuts**
168g	**soft brown sugar**
112g	**butter**
6tbsp	**double cream**

Preheat the oven to 180°C.

Begin by putting the chopped dates in a bowl and covering with 175ml of boiling water.

Then add vanilla extract, coffee essence and the bicarbonate of soda.

Cream butter and sugar until fluffy and pale.

Slowly add the eggs.

Fold in the sifted flour, then fold in the date mixture *(don't worry about it all being a bit sloppy, it is meant to be)*. Pour into a greased deep baking tin and bake in the centre of the oven for 25 minutes. Allow to cool and then run a knife around the tin and turn out. Slide onto a heatproof tray or plate.

Melt together all the ingredients for the sauce and allow to boil.

Pour over the pudding.

If time allows place under a hot grill for 4–5 minutes, this will warm through the pudding mixture and the sauce will bubble and soak into the pudding.

Serve with pouring cream.

Chocolate croissant bread and butter pudding

	butter, for greasing
2tbsp	**double cream**
4tbsp	**chocolate and hazelnut spread**
2	**free-range eggs**
2	**ready-made croissants**, sliced

To serve

icing sugar, to dust

double cream, for drizzling

Preheat the oven to 180°C.

Grease an ovenproof dish with butter.

Place the cream and chocolate and hazelnut spread into a large bowl. Crack in the eggs and whisk together until smooth and well-combined.

Arrange the croissant slices in the base of the dish and pour over the cream and chocolate mixture.

Transfer to the oven and bake for 10–12 minutes, or until set.

To serve, dust the pudding with icing sugar. Place servings of the pudding into bowls and drizzle with cream.

…And for something lighter…

Citrus fruit brûlée

1	yellow grapefruit
1	pink grapefruit
2	oranges
3	clementines
142ml	double cream
142ml	soured cream
56g	caster sugar
	lemon juice, a generous squeeze
84g	muscavado sugar

Peel the grapefruit and take the flesh of the fruit from each segment. Peel the oranges, remove all the membrane, then slice them into ¼ inch rounds. If the segments of grapefruit and orange are large, halve them. Peel the clementines but leave the segments whole.

Place the fruit in a flameproof shallow serving dish and spread the fruit out evenly.

Whip both creams together with the caster sugar and lemon juice, spread evenly over the fruit. Preheat the grill then sprinkle the muscavado sugar over the top. Warning; muscavado sugar burns readily, so do not place too close to the grill, and when grilling watch carefully for any areas that are catching. Have an oven glove handy! When evenly brown and bubbly, allow to cool then place in fridge to chill until serving.

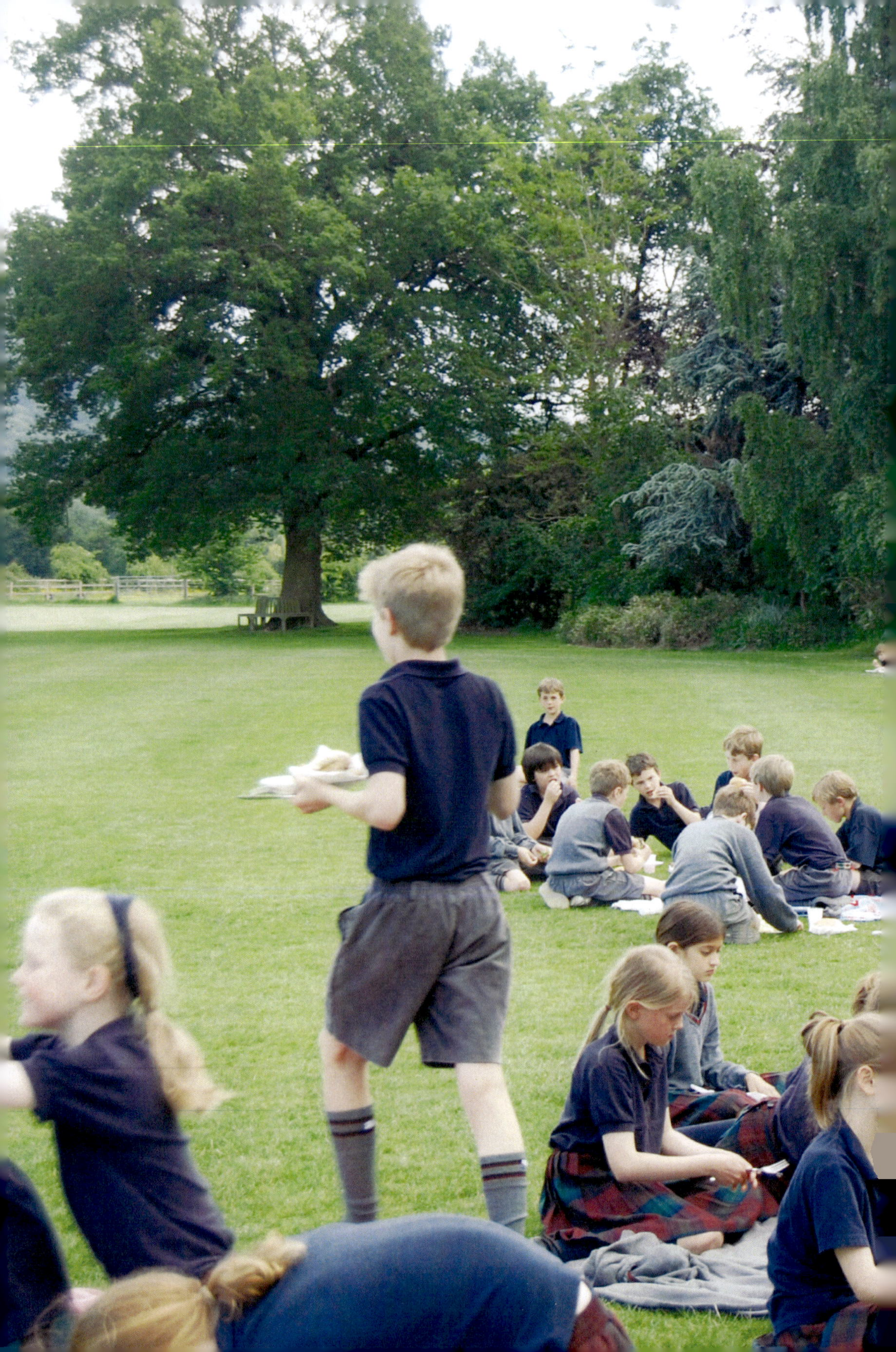

Summer Term

The Summer term encompasses many of the children's favourite pastimes. Some of the boys may argue that the Winter Term, and rugby, is the favoured term but the exuberance of the children in the Summer Term is very evident. There is a constant thump of balls landing on the pitches, cheers of delight are often followed by mutters of exasperation, to be heard from both girls and boys.

Rural Studies and 'The Garden' see many enthusiastic students earnestly tending their individual plots, rivalry is rampant (and even…sabotage).

Produce is abundant, every crop that is grown by the children, under rural studies master Grenville's patient guidance, is sampled by them. Salt, bread and butter are supplied for the young gardeners to create the most enviable 'double deckers,' containing carrots, radish, a variety of lettuce, cucumber, rocket, nasturtium flowers, peas and beans. Not only Mr McGregor, but also the Head Gardener at Highgrove, would be delighted by the care and reverence with which 'sandwich filling' is treated.

The produce from the Rural Studies garden is so abundant that a special summer feast is a new permanent fixture on The Elms' Calendar.

For those who are only happy if there is a slice of meat present on their plate, there is a Hog roast to accompany the assorted garden produce (inevitably, a 'close to home' Hog).

From the finest fillet of Elms beef
Carpaccio

100g	**beef fillet**, very finely sliced
2tbsp	**olive oil**
	maldon salt
2tbsp	**worcestershire sauce**
	fresh thyme

For the beef carpaccio, place the beef slices between two sheets of cling film and lay on a flat work surface. Beat out the beef slices using a meat mallet or rolling pin until very thin, then place the slices onto a serving plate.

Put the olive oil, salt and Worcester sauce into a bowl and mix well. Drizzle over the beef slices and garnish with a sprinkle of fresh thyme leaves.

To accompany Elms' beef and pork, the busy and inventive magicians in the school kitchen collude together to provide a wonderful range of salads. The end result can only be described as a veritable feast.

Fried cabbage with juniper

	savoy cabbage
1tbsp	**sesame seeds**
1tbsp	**juniper berries,** crushed
2	**garlic cloves,** chopped
	sea salt
2tbsp	**oil**
1	**red chilli,** deseeded and thinly sliced
2tsp	**sesame oil**
1tbsp	**ginger (fresh),** finely chopped
1tbsp	**runny honey**
	splash of soy sauce
	salt and pepper
	bunch of coriander, coarsely chopped

Chop the cabbage leaves into ribbons (removing the chunky heart). Fry the sesame seeds until brown.

Using the back of a spoon and a bowl, crush the juniper berries and garlic with sea salt.

Add the cabbage to the sesame seeds plus the juniper crushed mixture, turn up the heat and keep stirring for approximately 5 minutes, then add the honey, soy sauce, ginger, salt and pepper. The end result should be crunchy but not overcooked, at the very last minute stir in the chopped coriander.

Spring salsa verde

This is a lovely dressing or sauce which will act as a happy addition to cold meats or to liven up virtually anything savoury.

large bunch parsley

large bunch of herbs eg coriander, chervil, sorrel

4 gherkins

20 capers (approx.)

olive oil

1 lemon, juice only

salt and pepper

Chop the herbs fairly roughly, add the lemon juice, oil, salt and pepper. Give it all a thoroughly good mix.

Crushed peas

600g frozen peas

85ml olive oil

2tbsp mint, finely chopped

2tbsp parsley, finely chopped

salt and pepper

1 lemon, juice only

Pulse the peas in a food processor, be careful not to purée them!

Transfer the pulsed peas to a saucepan, add the olive oil, herbs and a good scrunch of salt and pepper.

Cook on a medium heat for a couple of minutes, then add the lemon juice. Make sure it is all thoroughly warm and serve.

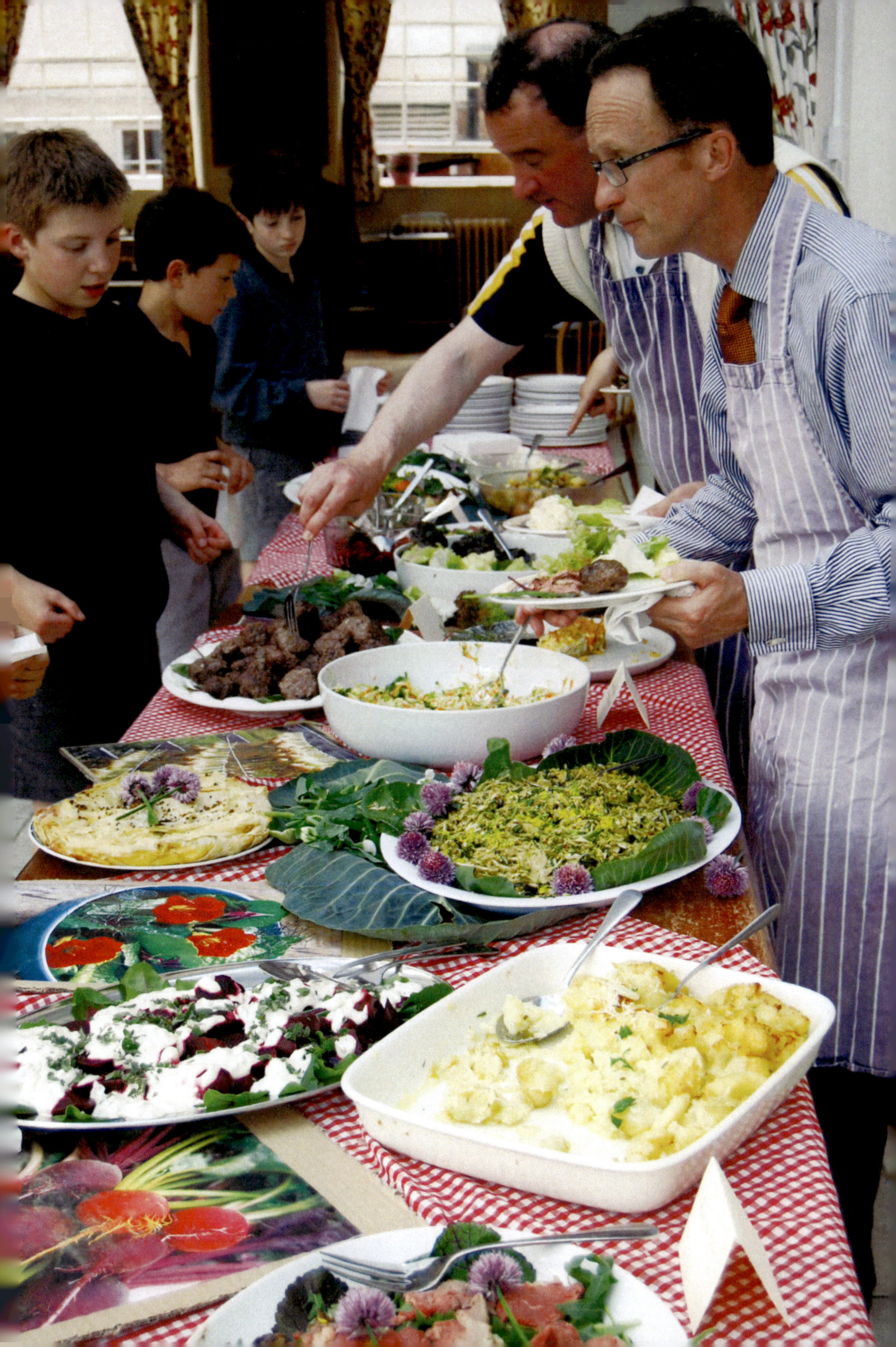

Smashed new potatoes with garlic and rosemary

1	head of garlic
1kg	new potatoes
1tbsp	rosemary finely chopped
50g	butter
3tbsp	olive oil
	salt and pepper
	grated pecorino

Preheat the oven to 200°C.

Put the whole garlic on a piece of foil and cook for about 40 minutes.

Scrub the potatoes and boil for about 15 minutes with salt.

Melt butter in a pan, squeeze out the garlic and add to the butter. Add finely chopped rosemary.

Toss the crushed potatoes in the garlic butter mix, season well, then drizzle with olive oil.

Place in an ovenproof dish and roast until golden brown and crisp.

Scatter with a layer of finely grated pecorino.

BASTILLE DAY

Later in the Summer Term Bastille Day is celebrated. Unfortunately it is not always possible to celebrate this piece of French history on the actual date but The Elms, with its famed enthusiasm, delivers a lunch 'à lá française'.

Les français apprécient énormement la gastronomie et pour les enfants des Ormes (the Elms), la journée française est une occasion de déguster les délices de notre cuisine à la française!

Escargots

tin of snails with shells 1 clove **garlic** **double cream** **parsley**	Drain the snails. Melt butter in frying pan, squeeze in a clove of garlic, toss. Add a gloop of double cream, plenty of chopped parsley and pop the snails back into their shells.

Followed by Normandy Chicken, needless to say without the addition of Cider, Calvados or Brandy!!

Normandy chicken

168g thick cut bacon, cut into ¾ inch dice

4 boneless, skinless chicken breast halves

50g plain flour

50g yellow onions, finely chopped

125ml calvados (or brandy)

250ml apple cider

375ml red apples, thinly sliced

125ml heavy cream

4tbsp butter, cut into pieces

1tbsp fresh thyme, chopped

fresh chives, to garnish

In a large, heavy saucepan, cook the bacon over medium-high heat until crisp and the fat is rendered, 4–5 minutes. Remove and drain on paper towels. Drain off all but 1 tablespoon of the fat.

Season the chicken on both sides with salt and pepper. Dredge in flour to coat lightly, shaking to remove any excess. Add the chicken to the fat in the pan and cook over medium-high heat until golden brown on both sides and nearly cooked through, about 4 minutes per side. Remove and cover to keep warm.

Add the onions and cook, stirring, for 3 minutes. Add the Calvados and cook, stirring, to deglaze the pan. Simmer until reduced by half. Add the cider, bring to a boil and cook until reduced by half. Add the apples and cook, stirring until tender, for about 2 minutes.

Add the cream and simmer until reduced by half. Reduce the heat to medium-low and add the butter, several pieces at a time, and cook, stirring, until each is incorporated. Stir in the thyme.

Return the chicken and any accumulated juices to the pan and cook until the chicken is heated through and cooked all the way, turning every 1 to 2 minutes.

Followed by…

Tarte aux prunes

450g sugar
900g plums
150g soft butter
200g self raising flour
3 eggs

To serve

your choice: crème fraiche, softly whipped cream, ice cream...etc.

Preheat the oven to 170°C.

Put 275g sugar plus 150ml of water in heavy based pan, stir until sugar dissolves, then allow to boil until it caramelises.

Halve and stone the plums.

Pour sugar mixture into baking tin suitable to contain the tart.

Place the plums face side down onto the sugar mixture.

Put the butter, remaining sugar and the flour into the food processor and whizz. As soon as the mixture holds together, spoon over the top of the plums and spread gently.

Bake in a pre heated oven for 1 hour. The centre should be firm to touch and the sides should be shrunken from the sides of the pan.

Allow to rest in pan for 5 minutes before flipping out.

GRANDPARENTS' TEA

Grandparents' Tea is a happy occasion when three generations come together to enjoy a 'Slap up Tea', hopefully, with weather permitting those, present are able to enjoy the wonderful setting of The Elms' gardens and, at the same time, take in the ever changing backdrop of The Malvern Hills.

Courgette and lime cake

250g courgettes
2 large eggs
125ml vegetable oil
150g caster sugar
225g self raising flour
½tsp bicarbonate of soda
½tsp baking powder

For the icing
200g cream cheese
100g icing sugar sieved
1 lime, juice only
2-3tbsp chopped pistachio nuts.

Preheat the oven to 180°C.

Grate courgette (with skin) on the coarse side of grater. When grated press into a sieve over the sink to remove the water.

Put eggs, oil and sugar into a bowl and beat until creamy. Sieve in the flour, the bicarbonate of soda and baking powder. Stir in the grated courgette. Pour the mixture into a 9 inch cake tin and bake for 30 minutes.

Allow to cool in tin for approximately 5 minutes, then turn out onto wire rack.

To make the icing, put sieved icing sugar into a bowl, beat in the cream cheese, add the lime juice and mix thoroughly. Spread on cake when cooled and sprinkle with chopped pistachio nuts.

Beetroot cake

200g	plain flour
¾tsp	baking powder
¾tsp	bicarbonate of soda
¾tsp	ground cinnamon
¼tsp	fine salt
50g	soft dark brown sugar
125g	light muscovado sugar
3	large eggs
½tsp	vanilla extract
300ml	vegetable or sunflower oil
225g	raw beetroot, peeled and coarsely grated (approx. 3 medium beetroot)
½	orange, zest only

For the icing

50g	unsalted butter, softened at room temperature
100g	icing sugar, sifted
½	orange, zest only
125g	cream cheese
	orange zest, for decorating

Preheat the oven to 180°C. Grease the loaf tin and line the base and sides with baking paper.

Sift the flour, baking powder, bicarbonate of soda, cinnamon and salt into the bowl of an electric mixer. Add the sugars.

Beat together the eggs, vanilla extract and oil and pour onto the flour mixture. Beat the mixture until smooth. Add the grated beetroot and orange zest and beat again. Pour the mixture into the prepared tin and bake on the middle shelf for 40 minutes. Turn the oven down to 170°C and bake for a further 20 minutes or until a skewer comes out clean when inserted into the middle of the cake. Leave to cool for 10 minutes and then remove from the tin and cool on a wire rack.

To make the icing, beat together the butter, icing sugar and orange zest until smooth and creamy. Add the cream cheese and beat again until smooth. Spread the icing over the top of the cake and decorate with orange zest.

Just so that you know.... This cake keeps incredibly well, it is best eaten a couple of days after baking, as it gets fudgier and fudgier. It also freezes (without the icing) very well.

Food is an important part of the Pre-Prep day. Small hands mix and mash. One of their favourite snacks believe it or not is...

Guacamole

2 **ripe avocados**, peeled and stoned

15ml **lemon juice**

30-60ml **olive oil**

1 **clove garlic**, crushed

5ml **fresh coriander leaves**, chopped

1 **large tomato peeled**, seeded and chopped

salt and pepper

Mash together or blend the avocados and lemon juice. Then mix in the garlic, coriander, olive oil and tomato. Season to taste.

The Summer Term rattles on at a rapid pace. Pupils in their final year have taken their scholarship and entrance exams to their chosen senior schools.

Leavers' Camp is the 'wind down' or more probably the wind up to the end of a hectic final term at The Elms. For those moving on, a special Leavers' Supper on the last night of term will be 'The Last Supper' that they will enjoy together.

Weather willing, this is eaten outside on the lawn.

Quick chicken liver pâté

175g unsalted butter, softened

450g chicken livers, trimmed and cleaned

2 shallots, finely chopped

1tsp soft thyme leaves

2 cloves garlic, finely chopped

2tbsp brandy

2tsp anchovy essence

½tsp freshly ground black pepper

55g clarified butter, melted

Heat 15g of the butter in a frying pan until foaming.

Add half the livers and fry for 7–8 minutes, or until golden-brown and cooked through. Repeat with a second batch of butter and livers.

Place the livers and juices in a food processor.

In the same pan heat another 15g of butter, add the shallot, thyme and garlic and cook over a moderate heat until the shallot is soft but not coloured.

Add the brandy, anchovy essence and pepper and scrape the bottom of the pan to release any coagulated juices.

Place everything in the food processor, including the remaining unsalted butter. Blend until smooth.

If you want a very smooth pâté, pass the mixture through a fine sieve and put in a bowl. Cover with the cling film, cool, then refrigerate. If not using within 48 hours, cover the top with clarified butter. *(Melted butter poured over in a thin layer, finely chopped herbs may be added, this is optional, it prevents the top of the pâté turning 'grey').*

Make some toast or have some nice fresh bread handy. Serve it all with a bit of greenery/radish/gherkins...and off you go.

Gazpacho

1kg	**ripe tomatoes,** roughly chopped (or three 200g tins chopped tomatoes)
1	**green pepper,** seeds removed, chopped
1	**small red onion or 6 spring onions,** chopped
½	**cucumber,** peeled
2	**large cloves garlic,** peeled and chopped
1	**small handful fresh basil leaves**
50ml	**extra virgin olive oil**
1 tbsp	**sherry vinegar**
	salt and freshly ground black pepper

For the garnish

1	**day-old baguette,** thinly sliced
	spring onion, finely chopped
	red pepper, finely chopped
	basil leaves

For the soup, place all of the vegetables, garlic and basil into a food processor and blend until smooth. Pass the mixture through a fine sieve to remove most of the pulp and skin, which you should then discard.

Lightly rinse the bowl of the food processor to remove any pulp and skin, then pour the sieved soup back into the food processor. Blend again, while slowly pouring in the extra virgin olive oil through the feeder, followed by the sherry vinegar, until well combined. Season to taste with salt and freshly ground black pepper.

Transfer the soup to a container and chill, covered, in the fridge until ready to serve.

For the garnish, preheat the grill to high.

Place the slices of baguette onto a baking tray and drizzle with olive oil. Season the baguette slices with paprika and salt, then toast under the grill for 1–2 minutes on both sides, or until golden-brown all over.

To serve, place an ice cube into each serving bowl and ladle over the soup. Float the crisp baguette slices over the soup, scatter over the finely chopped spring onions and peppers and garnish with a few basil leaves.

Insalata Isabella

1.4kg	chicken (approx.)
1	carrot, peeled
1	onion, peeled
2	celery stalks
2	garlic cloves, peeled
5 or 6	whole black peppercorns
	sea salt, freshly ground black pepper

Dressing

170ml	olive oil
2	lemons, juice only
100g	raisins
	celery stick
5tbsp	capers
	chilli, finely chopped
3	cloves garlic, finely chopped
	mint and parsley, chopped
2	frisee lettuce
	baby broad beans, lightly cooked
	spring onions, chopped

In 1489 this recipe was served to 500 guests at the wedding of Isabella of Arragon to Giano Sforza, an Italian nobleman… Fit for nobility, a fine choice for The Elms Leavers' Dinner.

Place chicken in a large casserole dish with the main ingredients; carrot, onion, etc., simmer gently in herbs and stock. Do not boil, or you will get a 'tough old bird'! When cooked, remove from casserole and allow to cool. When fairly cool, but not cold, remove skin, take flesh off bone and cut into fairly large strips.

Soak raisins in tepid water for half an hour.

Combine 6 tablespoons olive oil with juice of one and half lemons, add the chicken and toss. Add the capers, chopped garlic, the soaked raisins and the chopped chilli. Leave to marinade.

Just before serving add the chopped celery, broad beans and spring onions, mint, parsley and lots of salt and pepper.

Summer salad

10 ripe tomatoes	Quarter the tomatoes or cut in to 6.
2 white nectarines	Slice nectarines and mix together in a pretty bowl.
2 large balls of buffalo mozzarella	Break the mozzarella over the top.
2tbsp olive oil	Tear the basil leaves over.
2tbsp white balsamic vinegar	Mix balsamic and oil together, season and pour over ingredients in bowl.
salt and pepper	
bunch of basil leaves	

Elderflower and gooseberry ice cream

2 large eggs
50g caster sugar
200ml double cream
75g gooseberries
2-3 elderflower heads, plus a few heads/flowers to garnish
50g sugar

To make the purée, put the fruit and the elderflower heads into a pan with just enough water to cover the fruit, simmer very carefully until the fruit is soft. Push this mixture through a sieve when it is cool. Add the sugar; you may have to add a tad more, but the object is to have a sharp purée, not a sweet one.

Whip the egg yolks with the sugar until they are pale white and foamy, whip the cream and whip the egg whites until stiff.

Mix together gooseberry purée and the whipped egg yolk mixture.

Then add the cream.

Finally fold in the beaten egg whites.

Spoon the mixture into individual pots or glasses and freeze (or place in tub and freeze) but remember to take out of freezer at least 20 minutes before serving. Garnish with elderflower heads/flowers.

Lemon posset

570ml double cream
155g caster sugar
2 lemons, juice only

To decorate
fresh raspberries and/or blueberries

Bring the cream and sugar up to the boil in a large pan, stirring continually, otherwise the cream will 'catch' and burn…it is then a matter entirely for the bin…Use a really big pan and boil fairly hard as it rises up and remember to stir, stir, stir.

Boil rapidly for exactly 3 minutes.

Remove from the heat, whisk in the grated lemon zest and the lemon juice.

Plop three or four raspberries into the bottom of a small glass or coffee cup, allow the mixture to cool slightly, then pour it over the fruit. When set, decorate with more raspberries and a dust of icing sugar (the possets take a couple of hours in the fridge to set).

With full tummies the leavers then adjourn to watch a cleverly edited DVD revealing the highs and lows of their time at The Elms. There is much laughter, lively heckling and audience participation. Pathos does not escape. Strong friendships have been forged and challenges have been shared. Saying 'Goodbye' is never easy.

And for the Final Hurdle…

SPEECH DAY LEAVERS' LUNCH

Chicken with parma ham and goats' cheese

6 **chicken breasts,** one per person

baby spinach

goats' cheese

parma ham

olive oil

watercress, to decorate

Make an incision in the chicken breast, stuff the hole with baby spinach and goats cheese, wrap in Parma ham, drizzle with olive oil and bake in a hot oven for 20 minutes. Allow to cool, then slice and layer on a bed of watercress.

Tomato tarte tatin

900g tomatoes
2tbsp olive oil
sprig of rosemary
225g ready made puff pastry
large knob of melted butter
salt and pepper
basil

Halve the tomatoes and place them cut side up on a baking tray, drizzle with oil and season with salt and pepper. Place a few rosemary leaves on each tomato and bake for 25 minutes on a very low setting (70°C)

Remove from oven and increase temperature to 200°C.

Arrange the tomatoes in the bottom of a cake tin face side down, roll out the pastry and place on top of the tomatoes. Bake for 25 minutes. Leave to stand for quite a few minutes to let the Tatin have a breather, then turn out by holding a serving plate over the pastry and turning out 'like a jelly'. Season with sea salt and freshly ground black pepper and a few basil leaves.

Salmon in pastry with ginger

skinned and boned salmon, cut into two large fillets

shortcrust pastry

50g butter

stem ginger in syrup

dill, chopped

spring onions

salt and pepper

beaten egg

Mix butter, stem ginger, dill, spring onions, salt and pepper together in a paste.

Rollout the pastry to fit the salmon fillets.

Put one fillet on top of the pastry and spread with two thirds of the butter mixture.

Top with the remaining fillet and spread with the last of the butter mixture.

Parcel up the salmon in the pastry, brush with the beaten egg and bake at 180°C for about 40 minutes, until the pastry is golden.

This can be served hot, warm or cold... Perfect for a buffet.

Asparagus, pea and feta salad

150g feta
bunch of asparagus
handful of peas
handful of broad beans
bunch of rocket
salt
2tbsp olive oil
chopped parsley
balsamic vinegar

Blanch the asparagus for 2 minutes in boiling water, having removed any woody bits from the stalks.

Blanch peas and beans for 2 minutes. If the beans are bigger than your thumb nail, pop them out of their coats and they will make a much nicer salad.

Combine all the above in a bowl, drizzle with olive oil, a shake of pepper and sprinkle of salt and top with crumbled feta.

The Elms School entry into the

RHS MALVERN SPRING FESTIVAL
School Gardens Challenge

Title of challenge 'A moment in History'.

An apposite title for the four hundredth year of The Elms School.

APPENDICES

Appendix 1: Weights and measures

Weight conversion

1 cup = 200 grams (g)
1 ounce (oz) = 28 grams (g)
1 pound (lb) = 454 grams (g)
16 ounces (oz)
1 kilogram (kg) = 1000 grams (g)
35.7 ounces (oz)
2.2 pounds (lb)

Liquid measures

1 cup = 250 millilitres (ml)
9 fluid ounces (floz)
1 fluid ounce (floz) = 28.4 millilitres (ml)
2 tablespoons (tbsp)
6 teaspoons (tsp)
1 pint (pt) = 568 millilitres (ml)
20 fluid ounces (floz)
1 tablespoon (tbsp) = 15 millilitres (ml)
1 teaspoon (tsp) = 5 millilitres (ml)

Appendix 2: Abbreviations

°C = Degrees Celsius/Centigrade
°F = Degrees Fahrenheit
approx. = approximately
cm = centimetre
floz = fluid ounce
g = gram
lb = pound
ml = millilitre
oz = ounce
pt = pint
tbsp = tablespoon
tsp = teaspoon